PAST LIVES, FUTURE BODIES

PAST LIVES, FUTURE BODIES

kristin chang

Black
Lawrence
Press

www.blacklawrence.com

Executive Editor: Diane Goettel
Chapbook Editor: Kit Frick
Book and Cover Design: Amy Freels
Cover Art: "Night Mare" by Angie Wang. Used with Permission.

Copyright © 2018 Kristin Chang
ISBN: 978-1-62557-871-6

Published 2018 by Black Lawrence Press.
Printed in the United States.

Contents

Symmetry

How our bodies domesticate
           disaster: by swallowing

another country's rains. By reining
           my jaw to the sea, my bones

lurched into boats. My breasts bitten
           into apples. My mother says

women who sleep with women
           are redundant: the body symmetrical

to its crime. Between your knees
           I mistake need for belief

in a father figure: once, we renamed
           our fathers by burning them

out of our bodies, smoking the sky
           into meat. I have my father's name:

張, meaning archer.
           I consider coming clean

through you like an arrow. I consider
           the way we shape in bed, like the sea

has revised its shoreline & we
           the country it moves to meet. Every language

has different words for the same
　　　　　want. I name you the body

of water my thirst is native to.
　　　　　When I kiss you, I remember

every silence begins inside
　　　　　a mouth. Everything edible begins

as a bird. At night, birds peck
　　　　　peepholes into the dark

the way I have always
　　　　　watched women: in the distance

between a girl & herself
　　　　　is an entire body

bulls-eyed, arrowed
　　　　　holy. A girl castling

her voice into a throat
　　　　　of stone. I kiss you & forget

to turn on the dark. I taste
　　　　　salt afterward, trace

where light through a window
　　　　　veins your body, its wanting

to reroute your blood
　　　　　someplace safe.

The Chinese Sappho

To translate my mother
I swab her mouth

with a sword. I have never understood her
grief as grammar. She wants the plural of violet

to be violence, the plural of woman
omen. I knew the definition of damn

before dyke. I've never read *The Price
of Salt* & *Blue is the Warmest Color*

is so white I wrote it
this poem. Yes, I will always want

my mother more than a lover. But I still
dream of your breasts floating

over my head like furred moons.
I mumble your name with a bloodbent

tongue. Daylight defaces me,
shreds the eye. I lose more & more

face every time a white woman
compliments my eyes

I want to pluck them out, soft
boil them in their sockets & eat away

the whites. A tragedy that's Greek to you
is Chinese to me. Is there a difference

between wanting a country
to home & wanting a body

to hone? Don't tell me
I'll learn the language

it takes to know. Don't call 吴藻
The Sappho of China, don't forget Greek

was once a tonal language
like Chinese, it enters the body

slant. They say the mouth
shapes after its language.

My mouth ringing your nipple
is a vowel. In my dialect, every name

begins on a vowel, the mouth
circling itself. I circled your chest

like a restless bird, cribbing
inside your ribs. Your heart wringing

vowels out of blood. Over the phone
I teach my mother the difference

between singular & plural. I say
in English, the word changes

to match the thing. She says no,
a word is the thing itself: one woman

is a woman. Two, a woman woman.
Three. A woman woman

woman, she asks: when will you learn
to act the word? Like a mother's voice

I want to be beginningless.
I fantasize about my mother still

alive. Too soon
the tones of my birthname

sour like mourning
breath. When a word

is gone, the meaning
haunts the mouthhole.

When my body doubles
over, a ghost saddles

my back. The sum of my meat is
mare. The sum of my language

loss.

anchor baby

who will smuggle me
back into a body
        of   water
          is another way
          to say mass   grave

say   a broken girl is still
         right twice a day

          ask me for proof
          of parentage   I'll point

at the water
    your own face
        slurring the surface   show me
          a shipwreck resettled   by schools of fish
          a skeleton barnacled   alive again   ecology
          evolved from grief   death our new way
                  of life
    here my child
     threads her tongue
       through a needle
        stitches me a mouth   without sound
      I turn my tongue on   itself   swallow my own
          language   gilled to survive   a sea
        I boil
      the sea into steam
        sweet tea   I bruise a pearl

in my jaw   swill salt
until my mouth is scoured

stone   I followed
this country's
coast like a scent
to prey
I didn't listen
when they told me *stay*

away
I didn't anchor
the ship

I sank it

Yilan

In Taiwan the rain spits on my skin.
  I lose the way to my grandmother's
house, eat a papaya by the side of the road,

  papaya in Taiyu meaning wood
melon. My grandmother's house is wood
  & always wet, as if absence

holds water. As if drowning
  itself. My stomach oversweetens
on fruit, wears a belt of rot. Pre-

  typhoon heat coiling back
like a punch. I take a train from Yilan
  to Taipei, the same route

my mother fled when the Japanese came.
  By the side of the road, she saw a child eating
another child's face. What my mother

  ate during wartime: five flies boiled
wingless. The open sores of fruit & so
  much rain. Once, a girl gunned

down with her mouth full
  of milk. Once, my mother
bent to drink from another

girl's mouth. In Taipei, I watch bodies
syrup in my heat-slow sight. A blonde
      woman in an advertisement

for skin bleach, looking like
      my ex, looking like my first
-world face. I watched

      the typhoon from the 65th
floor of the Marriot, watched
      smaller buildings lean

like thirst to water. After, a salt scent
      inflecting the air. In my mouth, a sea's
accent. In Yilan, they will gather the dead

      parts of the trees & burn away
the rot. It was my grandmother
      who taught me to burn

only what you must, then water
      the rest. Who taught me
that a tree is a body

      through which water becomes fire.
In Yilan, my mother harvested sugar
      cane, dragon's eye, unidentified

limbs, small & sickling like fruit
      fallen before it is ripe. In another country,
my mother watches soap operas

in her native dialect, about time
traveling women who fall in love
        with Japanese soldiers. I dream about

being loved in another time
        zone. About meeting a woman here,
speaking in a Chinese that bursts

        apart our mouths like fruitpulp.
We will pretend it is love
        that lasts. I pretend not to know

what men do. What women
        remember. I understand the news
enough to know another typhoon

        is coming, another estimated body
count: infinite. According to the news,
        it is possible to predict violence

like a storm. I call my mother
        & she speaks to me in three languages
but names me in one: Kristin, meaning

        bearer of Christ. In my name, too many names
for god. Through the second typhoon,
        I sleep with my fist against my jaw,

wake with my teeth hitting ache
        like a surprise pit. I dream of telling
my mother I love her

country. I dream of telling
my mother I identify sexually as
        alive. Instead, I sleep

until evening, dream of frying
        Yilan in an oiled dark. When
my grandmother died, we were asleep

        in America, 15 hours behind
in the night, our bodies living
        her history. When she died, I imagine

all the trees did too. I imagine
        the trees I touch are new
generations of the same

        loss. I left Yilan while the sea still
boiled with stormbirth. In Chinese,
        typhoon is *tai feng*, sharing a word

with *tai wan*. A nation named
        after its greatest disaster. My body
named for what it bears, what

        it bares: this nation,
where nothing is still
        waiting to be saved

& the dead are still
                dying.

In Pine Bluff, Arkansas

my mother walks seven miles
     to the grocery store. a white

boy in a truck throws an egg
     in her face & it fries, yoking

her skin to sunlight
     a yellow that oils

you flammable. at the grocery store
     my mother miscounts her coins

& the cashier says chink
     bitch. all my mother's best

insults are animals: cow, cock, spineless
     fish we fry in our mouths. we spit bone

into cake batter. we ruin
     birthdays, sing in accents, slay

anthems silent. god the streak
     of blonde in our hair. my mother

says she can't believe
     we live with animals.

when the rain hums
     a hymn on our roof,

we dance. we sip
     storms. my throat

opens like an umbrella
     & I swallow stone

fruits. my mother spends
     hours in a field, bunching

grapes into fists. we get
     a break on slaughter day.

some animals bred
     for meat & others

labor. in this country
     I am both

the piglet & the butcher's
     hook it was born for.

The Movers

I moved in with you on a Monday.
        You hired the movers, two men
named after their village: Dǒng
        & Dǒng. Twinned like fists

the left one looks like my father:
        he drove a moving van for 20 years
in Texas, named every desert
        the Gobi & told stories of Yeye

riding winged camels.
        Now Yeye's skin is sun
scoured into a mirror
        we fog with our faces.

We forecast the weather
        today: Yeye's ghost steaming
the front windshield.
        My father squints to steer, slitting

the landscape like a throat.
        My brother & I fit in the front
seat & our father drives us
        to white people's houses, old

colonials, new Tudors.
        I am allowed to watch
as he teaches
        my brother to body

bag furniture, to drag chairs
        like women: by the legs.
At 12, my brother moves
        into a man's body: built to be

broken into. My father's back
        like a camel, humps peaking
under his wifebeater. Once,
        I tried following them into a house,

mock-Tudor with a doll sitting
        in the upstairs window. Every surface
inside held flowers & I counted
        the Chinese breeds: Peony. Orchid.

Chrysanthemum. Nothing
        lived in our house. Later,
my father beat me
        & my brother, too. He said

the communists taught us to share
        blame. My skin scatters like sand
beneath his touch. I bruise
        in the heat, imagine how things

grow in the desert: sand
        stammering out a flower.
In the Gobi, my father
        says, *all survival*

is vengeance.
        All light is a candy
coated knife. I move
        in with you on a Monday.

I watch Dŏng & Dŏng
        jostle a bed through our too
small doorway. They share
        a sandwich in our living

room, five-spice & pork.
        I wonder what they think, two
women but only one bed.
        I wonder if their village

is desert, dunes
        shifting like breasts
beneath a thin
        shirt. They wear

the same body: sanded
        skinless. I imagine them winged
& aloft, carrying
        nothing. You say *they could*

be brothers   & I say
                or maybe lovers.

Televangelism

(for Agong)

In Chinese, *ghost* rhymes
    with *expensive* & mother

misspends her mouth
    on prayer with no payback, no god

bending our sky like a back.
    What a daughter costs

a mother must pay
    out of body: she reaches

into her blood
    like a wallet, a wound

we eat out of. She says
    one man's daughter

is another god's revenge: a river
    lassoes our local church & my body

expires mid-prayer.
    I wear my blood

as bracelets & go sleeveless
    on Sundays. When it rains, I cinch

the flood around my waist
    like a miniskirt. Say we'll be better

mothers than our mothers. Say our fathers fit
        in our fists. When I microwave my mouth

a prayer boils over. My tongue
        tides. Mother heaps a houseful

of salt on our family altar, fills
        a bath & stripteases, teaches me

to do the dead
        man's float. In a church

made of bone, I boil
        a broth of fathers.

I season my wounds
        & wear them aloud, my blood

lungs. I pile salt into an anthill
        & crawl home. When it floods, we flee

on the backs of our brothers. We
        each a queen. We seek sweet

things, eat our stomachs
        starved out & sugared.

Agong dies after dinner, bladder
        come loose like a coin purse, piss

scattering like pennies
        on the bed. Make a wish. Fling

a coin into his mouth & a god comes
        true. Call a river a phoneline, my voice

snipped into silences. There is no country
        we can afford to bury our dead.

Mourning, too, is an economy
        of light. It was day when he died

& dark when I miscarried a moon
        into the wrong country's night.

We burned paper Chinese
        money & it was the first

time I've seen my face
        on something worth

something. No one tells me
        why we capitalize God

but never ghost.
        Never grieve.

Historical figure

In fifth grade, homework
was dressing up as a historical figure

most like our mother.
I chose Betsy Ross, the flag
seamstress, though my mother

sewed wholescale skirts & not stars
to colonize. She spent two
nights on my costume, bloomers

& a bonnet, an apron borrowed
from the butcher's & still blood
stiff. I curled my bangs & cut

a flag from my mother's first
qipao, the one she wore for the first
man who made her

a mother. In all my photos,
she is Catholic & bow
legged, a girl with god

galloping her
like a horse. Now my mother
says god is like marriage: both a lifetime

spent on your knees. At night
she prays while stitching me a crotch
cloth, the kind Betsy Ross

bled in, bore citizens through. At school
I curtsy to the flag, right hand renewing
my chest wound, left hand lifting

an axe to fell my family
tree. The seams of my dress
outrun my blood, my mother's

bed callused with her body.
She stays up late to spine
her bible with sky

colored thread, remembers the first
time she saw stars not sewn
to a flag: on a beach

in Yilan, my grandmother stewed
her daughters in the sea, prayed
they would boil up & stay

islands. Instead, they rowed
apart, salt whittling their spines
to oars, the sea dragged along

like a skirt. The moon tries on
tonight for size & we let out light
like a waistline. We pry back the sky

to spy the god raining us. Thirst
our theology. History
our unflagging hands

unstitching this country
along its rivers, this body
shrugging free of its seams.

How I became fatherless

We leave while he sleeps.
Morning bright as a beak
feasting my bones clean, my mouth gone
to call god. Every night my father falls
asleep with his hands wringing
the voice from my throat. A blood-thin song
trickling out of my mouth. I drive
across two states, counting roadkill, recording
my speed in miles
per dead thing.

                    *

In Nevada, my mother can't pay
for the motel, so we sleep at the bottom
of the empty swimming pool, hunger
carving our collarbones into deep
bowls. On every table in my father's house, a bowl
of fruit: dragon's eyes, unripe papaya, green
mango. He plunges his thumb into the tender
pulse of a pit, chews for hours. To make the sweetness
last, he tells us to 切开, 吃多. In my dreams, he's a soldier
stranded waist-deep in a wound & I throw him a hand
grenade. Now he smiles with rubbled
teeth, cavities clean as bulletholes. Asleep, he's still as a shot
& skinned animal. I pet his head, each hair black & needle
thick enough to draw blood. Once, I found
a single honeyed strand. He joked he was dyeing
into a tiger, black & orange, the color of a bruise

hunting its own
healing.

*

Some days, every hurt
feels like the first. Today crows
fall out of the sky & the ground stinks
of surrendered flight. Today I tear off
my clothing like scabs, walk naked
in public. In California, my first fatherless
home is infested with beehives
vibrating walls into muscle. Before bed,
I imagine bees laying eggs in my marrow,
waking up as a pool
of hip-thick honey. In the house
we left, my father is still
asleep, blanketed in bees.
His body the sweetest feast. I carry him
in my mouth like a fist
of sugar. I suck
until my teeth riot
with rot & I have nothing
left in my mouth to keep
quiet.

My grandfather spends his veteran's pension

on las vegas & a divorce
from my grandmother's country:
war-stripped & baring its dead

like breasts. Along the strip,
he buys two decks of playing cards,
one printed with blondes & the other

brunettes. Their breasts identical
bullseyes. When I find them in a drawer
of my father's DVDs, I mistake their nipples for pink

eye. I mistake blonde hair
for split-ended lightning, stiffen my spine
into a lightning rod: the shock snags on my mouth

& burns a hairless path to my crotch.
I steal one card from each deck,
slide them between mattress & sheet

each night pressing
my hips down harder
into my crime. The first time

I dye my hair blonde, I overbleach
my scalp boils over & I bald
a halo into my head. I cut it short

& my mother calls me scarecrow.
I dream every night of a field erupting
with red crows. I wake

swimming in a bloodstain
I can't trace back to a body.
On my first trip to vegas, I get green

carded at every bar. I watch dancers
breathe fire, lean close
enough to burn

bald, to smoke-stunt
the parts of me that fur, that fear
my grandfather

set himself on fire
in wartime, I wonder if burning
is how the body becomes a lesson

in flight, a lessening light: in the charred
dark of my room, I listen to the man next door
make love to his wife. I dream of her hair

like a field to lose my feet in. In bed, I grill
my ghosts, scorch the sheets & repeat
my grandfather's stories about peasants

who self-immolate before the city can
bulldoze their bodies. It is a riddle to burn
what is mostly water but still needs

to drink. Every morning, I watch the wife eat
a continental breakfast of one grapefruit & two
hardboiled eggs. I dye my hair

her color, bleach each strand
until it is static, a city blacked-out
of our bodies. I imagine us

in bed, halving egg after egg
& feeding each other yellow
yolks. Before making love,

I tape the playing card over my face.
I tape her mouth over mine, fist
my teeth & roll them like dice, gamble

god for this. Count each rib
a coastline, a beach tilled
by my tongue. We neon

the night, lick light off
skin like salt.
I pray for morning,

a way to wake
inside her
body.

Midas

I ate myself out of womb, slurped
     my umbilical cord like a noodle.
I was born barren
     bottomed like a bowl, so hollow I held
a week's worth of rain to spend on
     trees, dead things. Mother wore her stillborns
like a string wears beads: fetal heads
     the color & size of cocktail onions.
I imagined sucking them
     one by one. I spent all
my pennies on jawbreakers,
     thought the red flavor was blood
until I bled. My mother
     grieved each child longer
than it lived in her.
     When I was born, my father
said he was coming
     inside another man's
wife. A waitress at his restaurant, she
     wrapped spring rolls so tight they birthed
lettuce, beefbits, jicama.
     My father the frycook, his father
the same. Their hands so oiled
     everything they touched
flamed. Like Midas if Midas
     loved fire not gold. My mother burned
out years ago. My brother's still
     kindling, his girlfriends all

white & the same type
        of arson. When I was born
my father came
        like he wanted me. I ate his sex
euphemisms: oven loading, pie
        holing, a watched pot is like
a watched woman: never coming
        to a boil. In every mirror, I am a double
ended wick. A match to my mouth
        & ass. No smoke without a fire
to feed. No daughter
        without a dad to knead, to beat
into batter & fry
        gold with my touch.

The History of Sexuality

I. Education

upstairs   my grandfather unbuttons
his pants before prayer   pisses into an urn
of my grandmother's ashes   *to remind her*
who's still alive he says   they married
in reeducation   camp   their bodies fine
boned   as birdcages   how they survived
a decade   of drought: she drank   his piss
he drank it   back from her   sharing
one body's   worth of water   taking turns
at thirst   at the end   of the war   she bore
a boatful of boys   drowned   each in her mouth
grief   what we speak   grief the country
I was born to   be queen   give me a king
to kill for   my crown   my name   is my grandfather's
mouth misfiring   he shot off his own   leg
roasted the bones   fractioned out   the flesh
to feed his children equally   in this family
I am the fullest   woman   in a century

II. Anatomy

My mother......born from a mouth like thirst
My father........born like a bone from breakage
His father........a military man, mapping bodies

into countries   cunts   into cattle
I want a meatless marriage   a man to feed into

myself   to duck my hunger through
doorways   name my knuckles   what I'd kneel for
I know a girl   is nothing if not
first god   first time   I kiss a girl   I want
my murder over   mercy   I want a hurt
to rhyme   with my mother's   a husband
to bed together   then bury   I want
a wedding to dress up   in my best   blood
I'll invite   all the family   I've forgotten to name
here   in bed with her   I try to
remember   a Chinese word   for body
that does not   also mean   man
all language   learned before   birth
opened my mother   like a mouth
I've been married   twice   once
as the bride   once   as an animal
at the altar   of my own   sacrifice

III. Abstinence

Every night, my mother braids my hair
before bed, watches my father

out the window shooting squirrels
by moonlight. I wake with hair
smoking & coiled like a trigger
finger. Teach me to aim for a life

before mine. This body won't let me
out alive. Tell me who I need

to outbleed: Mother, butcher me
your braid thick as my waist.

Mother, I have only wanted
to live your body

through a boy's, to know you
through knives. How to say my body

is closest to yours when clothed
in the same man. When skinned by his
hands into history. When a girl
touches my cheek, tongue

solving the salt of me, I tell her I'm not
that way. I tell her no one

has ever touched my mother
this way & what happens
outside her body happens
outside mine too. What happens now

is motherless. What happens now in
my body means I am

alone.

My mother tells me to pray in Chinese

because 1 in 5 dead people is Chinese
& the more who hear you

answer you. Because even miscarriage has a mother
tongue, a name for itself that survives

being spoken, my name in Chinese meaning
beholden to brightness, meaning light

learns me like the lyrics to loss. My mother
belts my skin to song & I perch my blood

on her lips. I beg for the beating
of wings. With my god

sized hole for a mouth,
I wake our dead

in the beds we build of them: grandfather's
a mattress stuffed with live birds & a cow

we slaughtered for the color
its blood translates to: Eve's

appleful mouth, every storm I
clothed in the wrong country, mother

go where the weather is dressed
for you. Here: a typhoon where your tongue is

your tether. Where home is what you swallow
the keys to. You break the storm at its waist to pray

we survive our sky, our language a ratio of sound
to sacrifice, I eat the beaks off birds & grow one

in Chinese, I never forgave my teeth
for knocking like knees, for the way

I limped into English, leaned
on each word like a crutch, calling

my teeth my *eating bones*. When
I forgot a word, you fed it to me

in the wrong language. Forgetting
is the only language I've known

fullness through. Forgive me: I goggle
our gods green-eyed, trade in my name

for a nation I can answer to. I still
mistake poems for pyres, kneeling

for prayer. Give me a language I was born
before. Give me a map, my every prayer

mat. Speak my name
as ours. Say this poem

is Chinese & my language not
a leash but a lease

that's up. My mouth
free now & mine

yours.

Closet space

I know I'm godless when
my thirst converts water   into wasps, my country a carpet
                              I finger for crumbs. A country

my grandmother breeds
dogs instead of daughters   because only one can be called
                              home. I am trained to lose accents,

to keep a pregnancy
or cancel it out with   another man. My tongue is
                              a twin, one translating

the other's silence. Here
is my lung's list of needs: how to hold water
                              like a woman & not

drown. I want men
to stop writing &   become mothers. I promise this
                              is the last time I call my mother

to hear her voice
beside mine. I want   the privilege of a history
                              to hand back unworn

to grow out of
my mother's touch   like a dress from
                              childhood. Every time

I flirt with girls, I say
I know my way around   a wound. I say let's bang
                              open like doors, answer to

god. I unpin from
my skin, leave it to   age in my closet & swing
                              from the dark, a wrecking

ball gown. In the closet
urns of ashes: we cremated my grandfather
                              on a stovetop, stirred

every nation we tried
to bury him in was
a war past calling itself
one. I stay closeted with

him, his scent echoing
in the urn, week-old
ginger & leeks, leaks
of light where his bones halved

& healed. With small
hands, I puzzled
him back together. I hid from
his shadow in closets

his feet like a chicken's,
jellied bone & meatless.
His favorite food was chicken
feet, bones shallow in the meat—

When he got dementia,
he flirted with my mother
he mouthed for my breasts
like an infant

We poured milk
into his eyeholes
until he saw everything
neck-deep in white

the Chinese color
of mourning, bad
luck, though the doctor
says everything is

genetics. I lock myself in
the smallest rooms that fit
in my mind, my grandfather's:
a house we hired back from

fire. So I'll forever
have a mother, I become
a daughter who goes by god. I urn
my ghosts, know each by a name

my own.

I take my mother to the hospital

& the doctor says
        all medicine is white
lies & lying

face-down, my mother
        is bloodless, a chalk
outline against white

walls, her blood
        guttering the halls.
Sometimes

a doctor is a murder
        weapon & my mother
wears the hospital

gown like her sheathe.
        I carry all my teeth
in a jar of rainwater

& they swim circles
        around their hunger. As a child,
my mother was smoke

scarred, her throat scarved
        in factory soot. As a child,
she taught me how to jump

into gutters after a storm,
        the two of us standing knee-deep
in the street like islands

refusing to flood.
        After, we shared the bed
with our fevers,

floating in gutters
        of our sweat.
On my mother's

lungs, dark spotting
        the screen like a storm
forecast, distant

as the doctor saying
        there's nothing
you can do

that you can afford.
        The doctor buries his hands
blade-deep in her chest,

sleeves rolled to the hilt.
        His pockets the kind
my mother sewed

into jeans for a quarter each.
        After shifts, she bought me gumballs
I was too afraid to eat.

I carried them one by one
        until my palms stained
permanently sweet. Now

my mother & I don't speak
        in any language. Outside
it is raining. Later, I will juggle

the drops in my mouth
        like an alphabet. I will
remember she once said

rain is free as we ran
        through every gutter
in the city. Birth is a price

we'll pay till death, my mother
        says she carried me out of her
body like a briefcase. I didn't cry,

only opened my mouth
        in hunger, practice
for the day

the hospital calls me
        back to collect
my mother

like a mouthful
        of rain.

on loving a white woman

she compares / your breasts
to dumplings / so you learn / to butcher
yourself / bite-sized / bed a buffet
of blood types / only two
kinds of women / wear white
ghosts / and brides / and you are / bridled
her body / born the weight / of what it has
displaced / she calls you / her favorite genre
of hunger / the house / her mouth owns
in your name / maimed from her mother's
moan / dilating your throat / into a birth
canal / every day / you birth an apple
it has nothing / to do with eve's
apples are native / to asia / meaning paradise
belongs to your people / not hers
meaning paradise / was eve's / colony
of fruit / you named / sweet before any god
made garden / of her mouth / you overstay
like an accent / she can't origin / you
borrow a river / from the riverbank
become its god / for a day / fish it clean
of your species / named for / its meat
is your mirror / eve / ate the apple
believing in someplace / better
than a white body / she balances apples
on your head / turns paradise
into target practice / she shoots
you out of a tree / calls this discovering
gravity / this country / gardens itself

gone / apples greened / into grenades
she shakes / your limbs / bare / her appetite
a belly of heirs / descending / into your mouth
an apple / you ached out / you sowed
between your legs / a brownout
a night to plow / through
mourning / in every country
your body / learns to be
its own better / predator

Poem for my mother's cleaver

For a body, I barter blood
      hum, breastmilk, my bullet

fed mouth. My mother beheads
      a fish, feeds me the brainstem

bloomed. At night, she plants her knife
      in a pitcher of blood & grows it

the length of my life. In the backyard
      she severs a sapling, swallows its young

death & says a body
      becomes its own

coffin. Before burial, she stabs airholes
      into my chest, carves out my eyes

& replaces them with bullets
      or river rocks, anything to look

less like my father.
      There are so many ways

to be born: to split a bone
      among many bodies. To fish

for a father in the river
      my blood banks. In the kitchen, I stuff

a bird with its own feathers.
      Mother kneads meat into my shape

tenderizes my tongue
      & rubs in silence

like a salt. She teaches me
      to kneel for every meal

to let the man eat first, finish
      in you first. Then sop up

the blood, rinse out your
      mouth. A bed is an endless cutting

board. A sink is where
      a body floats when it wants to

be found. My mother says
      men are like knives:

there is no name
      for everything they can do.

She teaches me to hold
      a knife like a man's

hand, to teach it
      the depth of my body.

She tells me not
      to flinch when he hits

bone. My mother
       preserves her breasts

in bedside jars, slits her belly
       into a knifeblock. Before bed

she teaches me to sharpen
       my hand by scraping it back

& forth between my legs.
       By morning, I am hot

metal, my fingers whirring
       blades. Someday I will

feed my father
       to my hands, make meat

of men's minds.
       Saliva moating

around my body
       like blood

circling
       a birth.

天天

I trace my ancestry back to bed
wetters, heavy bleeders, all the ways
a body cannot contain itself. This country

a wound selling our blood
back to our bodies for a profit.
At birth, I delivered myself

dead, bled you my best
red dress to wed in. Sew me a train
to Flushing & I'll eat the city up

to its hem. I'll haggle with a fruit
vendor: my wounds for his
skinless. In this city, we all want

bodies we can't be
priced out of. In another city's
night, another Chinese girl

jumps from a factory window.
I draw a lake on the sidewalk
to land her. I draw her

bending to drink
this street like a river.
In Chinese, 天 means both

heaven & *sky*.
From a distance, a body
falling is nearing

its god. Call this prophecy: if white
is the color of surrender, white
people are flags of their own

defeat. Here's another: it's too late
for my face to be anything
but my father's first, my son's

next. God is what comes between
a girl & her grief. When a girl begs me
to fill her like a meal, I lift my hips

like a bowl to her lips. I cut from us
a cake. The word *cremation*
is so close to *creation*

& a body on fire is fire
armed. It is New Year's
Eve when I'm necking a girl

& don't become her
noose. The church chimes
another year I've outgrown

my god, my mother
rocking in my arms like a boat.
When I kiss her

on the wound, she scabs the sky
in blood & feathers, a bed's worth
of wedding nights. Night is our city's

shroud. Grief our
gasoline. Say heaven
is the sky with sleeves

our size. Say ghost
is the girl still missing
from me. My mother's third

language is my only. She wears me
like an earring wears
its hole. Wound me & I'll make it my last

name. I'll marry into
my body, grow it
a girlhood to go with

my best gown, your best
gallows. When the sea tosses
my mother's boat

like a bouquet, I catch her.
I wed a country & bear it
our lives.

Lessons from my grandmother

To safekeep a daughter, swallow her
at birth. What you can't kill, you eat
alive. If your daughter loves you, beat her
the color of water: every sea
she'll cross is her own
body. When you pray, god will return

your wounds unopened. When
you hunger, famine will fold away
your cheeks like chairs. A husband
will live in you like a housefire. Run out
of exits. Every body has an unmarked entrance
fee. Every man I let in, I paid for

in daughters. There is no difference
between birth & evacuation: both
mean my body's a bomb
radius. So no soldier follows us back
to our bodies, I eat our shadows
off the ground. Remember I lived

in your body before you did. Your blood
I bled first. Your mouth I starve from
still. Keep your gods
within earshot & your daughters out
of their range. My throat a rifle
loaded with rain, your mother

mending a drought with her aim.
Every bullet that missed me
named you its heir. Marry the soldier
missing both arms: let him ride you
down the aisle. Let him hold you up
like a noose. Think of death

as donating your life
to someone else who needs it more.
I have so many lives, I give them away
unworn. Bury me in my body
so I'll have something to eat
down here. Meat is a meritocracy

& I was born the best
to feed you. What can a man's hands make
that mine cannot
butcher? Hunger is my wife & I
its knife. Worship is my whetstone
& the wound my witness. I married

for meat, birthed my children
before I had breasts
to feed them with. Once, while my husband
slept, I threw all my children off a bridge
so I'd never be outlived. Below,
a rain-fattened river:

Your mother went in last, bobbed
once, hollow as a spent bomb.
Your aunts swam away, lived in schools
of silver fish, nibbled away
their own corpses. Now write me
the river's next move.

Tell me if I dive after
my daughters or if death
is the better mother. Tell me
if your mother is swallowed
out to sea & returns to me
a storm. Throw her

a storyline & fish her out
dry. You can revise this river
into myth, rebuild this bridge
backless: still every water
is mine to weaponize.
In every life, I hold your mother

hostage from you.
I drown her to keep you
unborn, not yet
named but already spoken
for. Not yet your mother's
but already mine.

Acknowledgments

Thank you to the teachers who helped me re-plant these poems in a place they'd grow: Cathy Park Hong, Rachel Eliza Griffiths, and Danez Smith.

To Ja: Thank you for the past-midnight draft swapping, the train rides, the rituals. You're already the best matriarch I know. To Maya: Thank you for fighting the boys with me.

Grateful acknowledgment to the editors of the following journals, where poems from this collection first appeared, sometimes in slightly different form.

The Adroit Journal: "Televangelism"
Diode: "The Chinese Sappho" (written after Eloisa Amezcua's "Teaching My Mother English over the Phone")
Frontier Poetry: "How I became fatherless" and "Poem for my mother's cleaver"
Muzzle Magazine: "Symmetry"
the Shade Journal: "Yilan" (winner of a 2019 Pushcart Prize)

Photo: Ja Bulsombut

Kristin Chang lives in New York. Her work has been nominated for *Best New Poets* and *Best of the Net*, and she has been anthologized in *Bettering American Poetry Vol. 3* and *Ink Knows No Borders* (Seven Stories Press). She is a 2018 Gregory Djanikian Scholar (selected by *The Adroit Journal*), the recipient of a 2019 Pushcart Prize, and a Resist/Recycle/Regenerate fellow with the Wing On Wo Project in Manhattan Chinatown.